COUNTRY ROADS

COUNTRY
ROADS

Exeter Books

NEW YORK

A Bison Book

PHOTO CREDITS

Alabama Bureau of Tourism and Travel: 44–45
Alaska Division of Tourism: 154 (bottom), 156–157
Orville Andrews: 108, 142–143, 164–165, 166–167 (left), 170–171, 172–173 (right), 178 (upper left), 178–179 (right)
Arkansas Division of Tourism: 154 (lower left)
British Columbia Ministry of Tourism: 145
Canadian Office of Tourism
  Mike Beedel: 150–151, 152–153, 158–159 (right)
  Egon Bork: 130–131 (left), 144, 168–169 (left)
  Alan Carruthers: 10 (upper left), 10–11 (right)
  Andrew Danson: 19 (upper right)
  Drie/Meir: 12–13, 14–15 (right), 16, 21 (upper right), 97, 154 (upper left), 158 (upper left), 162–163
  Allan Harvey: 137 (upper right)
  Bill McLeod: 17, 160
  Dilip Mehta: 161
  Bruce Paton: 14 (left), 147 (upper right)
  R Semeniuk: 154–155 (right)
  Pierre St Jaques: 32
  Diana Thorp: 18–19 (left)
Four-by-Five: 1, 2–3, 8–9, 22–23, 34–35, 36–37, 42–43, 88–89, 106–107
Florida Department of Commerce, Division of Tourism: 48, 49, 50–51 (right)
Georgia Department of Industry and Trade: 46–47, 52–53 (left), 62–63
C J Hadley: 108–109 (right)
Paul Horsted: 98–99, 192
Kentucky Department of Travel Development: 57
© Kerry Kirkland: 50 (upper left), 126 (upper left), 131 (upper left)
Louisiana Office of Tourism, Department of Culture, Recreation and Tourism: 53 (upper right)
Massachusetts Division of Tourism: 25 (top and bottom right), 41 (upper right) 58 (upper left)
The Reverend M J McPike Collection: 132–133, 138 (top left), 138–139

Michigan Travel Bureau: 7, 70–71, 74–75 (left), 76–77, 80 (bottom), 84
Minnesota Office of Tourism: 72, 73, 79 (upper right)
Montana Travel Promotion: 122–123, 124–125 (left)
Michael Murphy (TTDA): 116–117, 120–121
Nevada Commission on Tourism: 110–111
New York State Commerce Department: 24–25 (left), 26–27, 28 (upper left)
Oregon Travel Information Section: 146–147 (left)
Salt Lake Valley Convention and Visitors: 113
South Dakota Department of Tourism: 90–91, 92 (upper left), 92–93, 96, 102–103 (left), 103 (upper right)
Tennessee Tourist Development: 54 (upper left), 54–55 (right), 60 (upper left), 64, 65, 66, 67
Texas Tourist Agency: 118–119 (left)
  Richard Reynolds: 119 (upper right)
Utah Travel Council: 112
Vermont Development Department: 20–21 (left), 28–29 (right), 30–31, 33, 38–39, 40–41
Virginia Division of Tourism: 56, 58 (upper left), 58–59 (right), 60–61 (right), 68–69
Wisconsin Division of Tourism: 75 (upper right), 78–79 (left), 80 (top), 81, 82–83, 85, 86–87
Larry Workman: 169 (upper right), 174–175
Wyoming Travel Commission: 94–95, 100, 101, 104–105, 134, 135, 136–137 (left), 140–141, 148–149
© Bill Yenne: 4–5, 115, 125 (upper right), 126–127 (right), 128, 129, 167 (upper right), 172 (upper right), 176, 177, 178–179 (right), 180 (upper left), 180–181 (right), 182–183, 184 (upper left), 184–185 (right), 186–187, 188–189, 190, 191

Designed and Edited by Bill Yenne

Photographs selected by S L Mayer and Bill Yenne

Captioned by Timothy Jacobs

Pages 2–3: A school bus plies the well-worn road near a typical farm in the verdant, rolling countryside of Pennsylvania, which the Iroquois Indians called the 'Land of the Endless Mountains.'

Below: Cows grazing on a hillside, against the misty sky; this scene could be anywhere, but the locale is California's Sonoma County.

CONTENTS

INTRODUCTION

If you've ever found yourself walking down that long and lonesome road staring at the glow of the sun as it settles low over a small town nestled in the pines, on the bank of an old free-flowing river—then you may recall a time in your life when the words 'country road' caused a rising in your chest that made you want to return, and linger there. There is nothing so peaceful as a country road—one of those narrow thouroughfares that are delicately but indelibly etched on the landscape and the psyche of the nations of the North American continent.

This book that I am privileged to introduce is a wondrous treasury of those roads that time forgot, yet are timeless and which will outlast in our fond memories even the grandest superhighways. The great railroads and highways of North America may be the bands that hold the continent together, but country roads run deep into the very substance of these great lands. These are the two-lane blacktops and gravelled ruts that lead us nowhere and yet everywhere.

Like the end of an age, like a sunrise, that clear watercourse of memory winds its way along the canyons, past buttes and cacti that seem to hover there, in the high desert heat, their bases separated momentarily from the cares of the Earth. Stay awhile, then follow. . .

Somewhere in the Northwest, an Indian fisherman tends to his mussel traps, and it reminds me of the time I sat and listened to a seasoned and cheerful fisherman, as he mended his nets and spun out tales of terror and sheer joy—the legends of a lifetime on the sea—years ago, and thousands of miles past in my own journey.

I remember the welcome hiss of the big rig's air brakes at sunset as the weathered truck driver delivered me from a blistering hitch-hike across the Oklahoma hills. He knew—and told me so—that the essence of the country road is one in sameness with the soul of this, the greatest of all great lands.

Beside crashing waterfalls, in the stillness of midday on the bayou, atop the spectacular beauty of the sheer rock cliffs, I stood and marveled, somewhere in the heavenly reaches of this continent and the tiny road that took me there.

That twister I saw dancing beneath a black cloud from the shelter of a Kansas farmhouse—it was the same, somehow, as the biting winds I was glad to be out of when the blizzard hit, and found that shack in Alaska. Or that wonderful mansion, remnant of another time—the warm courtesy the master of the house showed me when I stopped for directions in Georgia. . . it made me think of home, that little house by the brook, where the weeds and flowers intertwined in loving casualness, thanks to the kindly ministrations of dad's increasing fondness for things that grow of their own accord, and things that grow because we want them to.

I can remember so many times during the autumns I spent in Michigan, when renewal of a youth's fragile spirit meant a long drive up the Huron River Valley—alone with my thoughts, alone with *my* country road.

Here it is, a compendium of fondness, a photo album of another time that is yours to live. You need only set out on that small, buckled thoroughfare that is somewhere in your neighborhood, just down the block; a pathway to the wind, the sunshine and the rain—that country road that is, actually, best not forgotten, as its cleansing meanders strip away all that obscures your way.

It may not have been the longest that I've travelled, but the country road that will remain the longest in my memory is that narrow two-rut lane to Grandma's house. That last time, her lilacs were still there, but all was strangely silent. The low picket fence nodded sagely in the breeze, its roots softening in the soil.

—*William Patrick Jennings*

At right: In a favorite landscape for Sunday tourists, autumn leaves bedeck a road in rural Michigan. The air, so pure and crisp, is an invisible partner to nature's vibrant change-of-season display.

THE NORTHEAST

SPRING

The Spring is here, the delicate-footed May,
 With its slight fingers full of leaves and flowers;
And with it comes a thirst to be away,
 Wasting in wood-paths its voluptuous hours;
A feeling that is like a sense of wings,
Restless to soar above these perishing things.

We pass out from the city's feverish hum,
 To find refreshment in the silent woods;
And nature, that is beautiful and dumb,
 Like a cool sleep upon the pulses broods;
Yet, even there, a restless thought will steal,
To teach the indolent heart it still must *feel*.

Strange, that the audible stillness of the noon,
 The waters tripping with their silver feet,
The turning to the light of leaves in June,
 And the light whisper as their edges meet:
Strange, that they fill not, with their tranquil tone,
The spirit, walking in their midst alone.

There's no contentment in a world like this,
 Save in forgetting the immortal dream;
We may not gaze upon the stars of bliss,
 That through the cloud-rifts radiantly stream;
Bird-like, the prisoned soul *will* lift its eye
And pine till it is hooded from the sky.

——*N P Willis*

Previous page: A two-lane blacktop wends through a postcard-perfect New England village. *Above:* The sun shines on this modern-day Anne of Green Gables as she walks among the daisies on Canada's Prince Edward Island. *Right:* In a classic composition, on Prince Edward Island, flower garden, farmhouse and outbuildings are framed by rows of crops *(foreground)* and the Atlantic Ocean beyond.

AN ANCIENT CHURCH

Its stony sides are mossy-green with age,
  And round them rest the molded sepulchers
  Of many sacrificing characters—
The sainted hero, patriot and sage.
Archaic tablets on the walls engage
  Our solemn contemplation, and refer
  With love to each departed worshiper
As having earned a higher heritage.

We feel an awesome presence in the room
  Not classified or clearly understood;
Then, wondering beside a marble tomb
  Why all must join the silent brotherhood,
We leave the atmosphere of sacred gloom
  To hold communion with the living good.

——Willis Hudspeth

Below: Winding near this country church—dignified, and endowed with Prince Edward Island's Atlantic sunlight—a rural road leads travellers to the awareness that spring is in the air, as a sunset overcast betrays the abundant water that is—especially at this location—everywhere.

A QUIET COVE

There is a quietude pervading here—
   In charming contrast to the jangling crowd—
   Where Nature, tranquilized, communes aloud
In silent words to one's receptive ear.
The tide is turning, noiselessly and clear;
   A man with horses in a resting cloud
   Has imaged in the zenith, mantled, bowed,
Translated like the zealous Tishbite seer.

It represents a radio recess,
   Wherein retreating prophets may relieve
Their purposes from turbulence and stress—
   A station in attunement to receive
The message of the greater peacefulness
   Of thought from every stormy soul's reprieve

——Willis Hudspeth

Above: A fair sky and fishing vessels grace this view of New London Bay, Prince Edward Island. *Right:* A picnic is the festive focus of these travellers to Quebec's Gaspé Peninsula.

"HOW CHEERY ARE THE MARINERS!"

How cheery are the mariners—
  Those lovers of the sea!
Their hearts are like its foaming waves,
  As bounding and as free.
They whistle when the storm-bird wheels
  In circles round the mast;
And sing when deep in foam the ship
  Ploughs onward to the blast.

What care the mariners for gales?
  There's music in their roar,
When wide the berth along the lee,
  And leagues of room before.
Let billows toss to mountain heights,
  Or sink to chasms low,
The vessel stout will ride it out,
  Nor reel beneath the blow.

With streamers down and canvass furled
  The gallant hull will float
Securely, as on inland lake
  A silken-tasselled boat;
And sound asleep some mariners,
  And some with watchful eyes,
Will fearless be of dangers dark
  That roll along the skies.

God keep those cheery mariners!
  And temper all the gales
That sweep against the rocky coast
  To their storm-shattered sails;
And men on shore will bless the ship
  That could so guided be,
Safe in the hollow of His hand,
  To brave the mighty sea!

——*Park Benjamin*

Above: His own father a man of the sea, this dapper fisherman nods his welcome to those who would visit his 'home port'—North Rustico, on Prince Edward Island. For those who have the wisdom to pause awhile and linger, he may perhaps open his memory's treasure chest—and what stories he has to tell!

Right: With their backs to Newfoundland's Trinity Bay, these boys shyly pose to have their picture taken. They will no doubt learn their fathers' trade—riding the mighty Atlantic in search of living bounty—and after decades as fishermen, what might they teach *their* children; what stories might *they* tell?

A SEAMAN'S SONG

Like a ship I am gliding away
In a calm to a beautiful bay,
    Then astride the mane
    Of a hurricane
I am foundered in anxious delay.

Like a ship I am journeying home,
In repair from a perilous roam,
    Where the sleepy haze
    Of the rural ways
Will impel me again to the foam.

So hurrah for the rocks and the shale!
Like a ship that is ripping her sail,
    I shall find my ease
    In the surging seas,
With the petrels that sing in the gale.

——*Willis Hudspeth*

Left: Gambrel roofs and a church in the background give this Cavendish Beach setting an archetypal Atlantic seaboard appeal. Newfoundland has been the island home of many generations of fishermen such as these *(above)*, photographed at Petty Harbor.

from
JUNE

I gazed upon the glorious sky
    And the green mountains round;
And thought, that when I came to lie
    Within the silent ground,
'Twere pleasant, that in flowery June,
When brooks sent up a cheerful tune,
    And groves a joyous sound,
The sexton's hand, my grave to make,
The rich, green mountain turf should break.

A cell within the frozen mould,
    A coffin borne through sleet,
And icy clods above it rolled,
    While fierce the tempests beat—
Away!—I will not think of these—
Blue be the sky and soft the breeze,
    Earth green beneath the feet,
And be the damp mould gently pressed
Into my narrow place of rest.

There, through the long, long summer hours,
    The golden light should lie,
And thick, young herbs and groups of flowers
    Stand in their beauty by.
The oriole should build and tell
His love-tale, close beside my cell;
    The idle butterfly
Should rest him there, and there be heard
The housewife-bee and humming bird.

And what, if cheerful shouts, at noon,
    Come, from the village sent,
Or songs of maids, beneath the moon,
    With fairy laughter blent?

——*William Cullen Bryant*

Left: Summer warmth lights this lush New England farm, nestled in the cozy round-shouldered hills of Vermont. The old yellow lines of the 'two lane' lead the traveller through miles of beauty on Prince Edward Island *(above)*.

As the 'cold Atlantic' breaks evenly on the shore, beguiling sunset light lends warmth to this Cape Cod, Massachusetts evening scene. The little lighthouse that guards this stretch of coast has witnessed much beauty, and weathered much fury.

THE INDIAN SUMMER

What is there saddening in the autumn leaves?
Have they that 'green and yellow melancholy'
That the sweet poet spake of?—Had he seen
Our variegated woods, when first the frost
Turns into beauty all October's charms—
When the dread fever quits us—when the storms
Of the wild equinox, with all its wet,
Has left the land, as the first deluge left it,
With a bright bow of many colours hung
Upon the forest tops—he had not sighed.

The moon stays longest for the hunter now:
The trees cast down their fruitage, and the blithe
And busy squirrel hoards his winter store:
While man enjoys the breeze that sweeps along
The bright, blue sky above him, and that bends
Magnificently all the forest's pride,
Or whispers through the evergreens, and asks,
'What is there saddening in the autumn leaves?'

——*John G C Brainard*

Left: This panoramic viewpoint on Prospect Mountain, in New York State, provides a site for a friendly roadside chat. 'Reflected Fire' *(top of page)* and 'The Path of Autumn' *(above)* could be painterly titles for these photos taken in Massachusetts.

from
ON THE OLD FARM

Far away on the dear old farm
Is a home with a lasting charm,
    Old and gray;
Its roof with moss is covered
Where the waving branches hovered
    Many a day.

How often has the dawning
Of a beautiful June morning,
    Long ago,
At my window blushed while telling
Of the roses sweetly smelling,
    Just below.

The beauty, like a blessing,
Of Nature, sweet, caressing,
    Filled the air;
The woods and fields were glorious,
And summer reigned victorious
    Everywhere.

In meadows sweet with haying
We, happy children playing,
    Wandered free;
The birds sang gaily o'er us
While we would join the chorus,
    Full of glee.

——*Benj F Brown*

The old Eastern mountains acquiesce into farmland in this photo taken near New York's Interstate 88. Such placid vistas as this can be seen anywhere in upstate New York and Pennsylvania—both particularly mellow along US Route 15.

from
OCTOBER WOODS

What mortal brush can duplicate
   An autumn sylvan sight,
Or skillfully originate
   Such colors of delight?
No simulating human hand
Can make a piece of art as grand.

An arc of sumacs lines the grove
   With scarlet, in the rear;
Leaves—orange, greenish, buff and mauve,
   Red, auburn, soft and sear—
Hang quaking in the languid breeze,
Or, quiet, shine around the trees.

A woodbine clings against an oak,
   Beneath whose stalwart arms
The acorn and the artichoke
   Display their chestnut charms,
The walnut and the hickory
Commingling in the harmony.

The stretching clouds' tranquillity
   Blends with the turquoise hue,
And fills us with an ecstasy
   Which thrills us through and through.
He only, who depicted all,
Can truly paint a woodland fall.

          ——*Willis Hudspeth*

Above: A scene in an upstate New York village, delightfully cluttered with trees, could be repeated in any of the Eastern States. This little farm *(right)* nestles gently in the fall landscape of Woodstock, Vermont.

Covered bridges like the one below in Arlington, Vermont, have considerable charm, and have a much-honored place in American folk culture.

from

THE LAST DAYS OF AUTUMN

Now the growing year is over,
  And the shepherd's tinkling bell
Faintly from its winter cover
  Rings a low farewell:
Now the birds of Autumn shiver,
Where the withered beech-leaves quiver,
Over the dark and lazy river,
  In the rocky dell.

Now the mist is on the mountains,
  Reddening in the rising sun;
Now the flowers around the fountains
  Perish one by one:
Not a spire of grass is growing,
But the leaves that late were glowing,
Now its blighted green are strowing
  With a mantle dun.

Now the torrent brook is stealing
  Faintly down the furrowed glade—
Not as when in winter pealing,
  Such a din is made,
That the sound of cataracts falling
Gave no echo so appalling,
As its hoarse and heavy brawling
  In the pine's black shade.

Darkly blue the mist is hovering
  Round the clifted rock's bare height—
All the bordering mountains covering
  With a dim, uncertain light:
Now, a fresher wind prevailing,
Wide its heavy burden sailing,
Deepens as the day is failing,
  Fast the gloom of night.

Slow the blood-stained moon is riding
  Through the still and hazy air,
Like a sheeted spectre gliding
  In a torch's glare:
Few the hours, her light is given—
Mingling clouds of tempest driven
O'er the mourning face of heaven,
  All is blackness there.

——*James G Percival*

Above: Boating on Quebec's Gatineau River amid the evergreens and autumn leaves is a twofold pleasure, indeed. The dry leaf-crackling footsteps of animals and fellow travellers, serenity of wind powerfully whispering through trees and the sheer, meditative delight of being on or near vibrant, free-flowing water is quite beyond any notion save that of a gift given—and gratefully received.

Right: This village scene from another era greets the traveler along the Waits River in Vermont. The spiritual value of the simple, strong presence of the church commingles with the hearty utility of the barns and toolshed, to grant this place a sense of hard work done—both seen and unseen. Well-crafted houses add the final touch to a sense of communal depth which calls and beckons.

Above: This tree-lined lane has an air of stately quietude, in the meditative light of a late Ontario afternoon

A LIGHTHOUSE

A signal flashes warning from a tower
   Built on a promontory, massive, rough;
   The billows beat ferociously a chough
Against a ray that streaks the midnight glower.
Black danger hovers in the sullen hour;
   A pilot, sturdy, resolute and gruff,
   Observes another craft in time to luff
His own to safety with prodigious power.

In this way does the public beacon flash
   Us admonition on the sea of trade,
Where partial interests are prone to clash
   In war, intrigue and private ambuscade.
We struggle onward in the waves that lash
   Us till the light of reason is obeyed.

——*Willis Hudspeth*

Below: The strong, steady light from this lighthouse presides over the highways, byways and waterways of Fire Island, across the Great South Bay from Long Island's southern shore.

A covered bridge, built to fend off the elements on all sides, gives this country lane *(below)* near East Montpelier, Vermont a respite from the early winter's snow.

WINTER

How the wind whistles and rattles the blinds
  While the rain and sleet strike the window panes,
And the Storm-King marshals his hosts and finds
  Every place where a hole or crevice remains.

The snow sifts in when the gusts fly past,
  The drifts whirl over the garden wall,
The storms of winter are here at last
  Draping the sky with a leaden pall.

The back-log lies in the wide fireplace,
  And the burning embers search its heart,
While the glowing fire creeps on apace,
  Tearing its sinews of oak apart.

Let the storm go on, we defy the cold,
  We are cosy and warm in the lamp-lit room,
While apples roast in the ashes old
  And the walnuts crack to meet their doom.

We gather around the fireside now
  And talk of the days in the long ago,
Of the glorious times we had and how
  We would race our steeds over ice and snow.

Let the winter come, there are joys it brings
  To the boys and girls, to the young and old:
Every snow-clad hill in the moonlight sings
  Of the 'mansions fair and the streets of gold.'

——*Benj F Brown*

Left: The snowplows have 'just the day before' cleared this thoroughfare near Albany, Vermont. *Above:* Cross-country skiers pass through a rustic barnyard in rural Massachusetts.

THE ROAD NOT TAKEN

Two roads diverged in a yellow wood,
And sorry I could not travel both
And be one traveler, long I stood
And looked down one as far as I could
To where it bent in the undergrowth;

Then took the other, as just as fair,
And having perhaps the better claim,
Because it was grassy and wanted wear;
Though as for that the passing there
Had worn them really about the same,

And both that morning equally lay
In leaves no step had trodden black.
Oh, I kept the first for another day!
Yct knowing how way leads on to way,
I doubted if I should ever come back.

I shall be telling this with a sigh
Somewhere ages and ages hence:
Two roads diverged in a wood, and I—
I took the one less traveled by,
And that has made all the difference.

——*Robert Frost*

THE SOUTH

Previous page: An antebellum mansion waits across the lawn as Miss Melanie comes to greet you 'by the roadside' in Alabama. *Below:* This classic Southern scene, posies in the foreground and porch-fronted grocery offering its shade, sings its gentle blues to the traveller in Pine Mountain, Georgia.

from
NATURE'S SONG OF GEORGIA

Down in sunny southland
Nature tells the story
Of its treasure storc in Georgia
That is yet to claim great glory.

The wind goes whispering through the
trees
And bids them be content,
So good and greatly woods
Shall give the Nation recompense.

The sun and wind agree
That since ole Georgia has a share
In most of Nature's royal gifts
That they put all their climates there.

Georgia gives so many themes
For the birds to sing about;
Songsters stay the whole year through—
Then they never sing them out.

——*Vera McElveen*

ALONG THE RIVER BANKS

Along the river banks we wandered, you and I,
Full happy in today and thoughts of by and by;
Above the shaded path the gentle summer breeze
Seemed whispering a song amid the rustling leaves.

Along the river banks we wandered, you and I,
The brightest day in June, beneath a cloudless sky;
The river glided on 'twixt banks of emerald green,
Bedecked with lovely flowers, kind Nature's smile serene.

Along the river banks, I never can forget
Those happy hours we spent in memory linger yet;
Upon the bank we sat, charmed with the summer night
Born of the sunset rays and fading soft twilight.

Along the river banks, 'twas in the long ago,
And there we made our vows, together we would go
Along the stream of life, each in each other's care,
Contented on our way, all joys and griefs to share.

——*Benj F Brown*

Left: The 'Boys of Summer' were once you and I: Blue Springs offers this idyllic 'swimmin hole scene'—yet another of Florida's abundant treasures—especially precious in the Southern heat.

A tattered curtain of Spanish moss bedecks this view of Tallahassee's Lake Hall *(above)* making it into nature's version of a huge, wax-floored ballroom in a torpid Southern mansion: one good reason for a mint julep.

OLD-FASHIONED LETTERS

Old-fashioned letters! How good they were!
    And nobody writes them now;
Never at all comes in the scrawl
On the written pages which told us all
The news of town and the folks we knew,
And what they had done or were going to do.
    It seems we've forgotten how
To spend an hour with our pen in hand
To write in the language we understand.

Old-fashioned letters we used to get
    And ponder each fond line o'er;
The glad words rolled like running gold,
As smoothly their tales of joy they told,
And our hearts beat fast with a keen delight
As we read the news they were pleased to write
    And gathered the love they bore.
But few of the letters that come to-day
Are penned to us in the old-time way.

Old-fashioned letters that told us all
    The tales of the far away;
Where they'd been and folks they'd seen;
And better than any fine magazine
Was the writing too, for it bore the style
Of a simple heart and a sunny smile,
    And was pure as the breath of May.
Some of them oft were damp with tears,
But those were the letters that lived for years.

Old-fashioned letters! How good they were!
    And, oh, how we watched the mails;
But nobody writes of the quaint delights
Of the sunny days and the merry nights
Or tells us the things that we yearn to know—
That art passed out with the long ago,
    And lost are the simple tales;
Yet we all would happier be, I think,
If we'd spend more time with our pen and ink.

——*Edgar Guest*

Above: Seeming to compose this very beautiful scene, which is truly 'visual poetry,'
a cherry branch brings life to the folk phrase, 'Sweet Home Alabama.' *Right:*
Ochopee, Florida boasts this, the smallest post office in the United States. They build
things bigger in Mississippi—as is attested to by Eudora Welty's story, 'Why I live
at the PO.'

CONTINUATION

Incessant tropic winds that pass
   Bestir the grass,
And whisper in the autumn calm
   The shepherd's psalm
Of life beyond the somber scene,
Where pasture fields are always green.

Nearby enduring blossoms shine
   From out a mine:
The ruby and the rhodolite
   Without a blight;
The purple, red and yellow quartz
That bloom for ages in the arts.

And, nearer still, a runlet sings
   Of hidden springs;
The constancy of their supply
   That falls from high.
Is't Immortality that speaks
This faith through zephyrs, rocks and creeks?

     ——*Willis Hudspeth*

Left: Tiger lilies give a distinctly Southern charm to this view of a Roswell, Georgia mansion. *Above:* The sun seems to rest among the limbs of this cypress tree, at day's end on Louisiana's Lake Palourde.

from

AUTUMN EVENING

Go forth at eventide,
When sounds of toil no more the soft air fill,
When even the hum of insect life is still,
    And the bird's song on evening's breeze has died;
Go forth, as did the patriarch of old,
And commune with thy heart's deep thoughts untold,
Fathom thy spirit's hidden depths, and learn
The mysteries of life, the fires that inly burn.

Go forth at eventide,
The eventide of summer, when the trees
Yield their frail honours to the passing breeze,
    And woodland paths with autumn tints are dyed;
When the mild sun his paling lustre shrouds
In gorgeous draperies of golden clouds,
Then wander forth, mid beauty and decay,
To meditate alone—alone to watch and pray.

Go forth at eventide,
Commune with thine own bosom, and be still,
Check the wild impulses of wayward will,
    And learn the nothingness of human pride;
Morn is the time to act, noon to endure;
But, O! if thou wouldst keep thy spirit pure,
Turn from the beaten path by worldlings trod,
Go forth at eventide, in heart to walk with God.

——*Emma C Embury*

Above: A champion quality is evident in this fine colt, walking so regally through the Tennessee autumn. *Right:* Amid the color burst of dying leaves, a mare and her foal accept a tidbit offered by these boys *(right).*

MY PAW SAID SO

Foxes can talk if you know how to listen,
    My Paw said so.
Owls have big eyes that sparkle an' glisten,
    My Paw said so.
Bears can turn flip-flaps an' climb ellum trees,
An' steal all the honey away from the bees,
An' they never mind winter becoz they don't freeze;
    My Paw said so.

Girls is a-scared of a snake, but boys ain't,
    My Paw said so.
They holler an' run; an' sometimes they faint,
    My Paw said so.
But boys would be 'shamed to be frightened that way
When all that the snake wants to do is to play;
You've got to believe every word that I say,
    My Paw said so.

Wolves ain't so bad if you treat 'em all right,
    My Paw said so.
They're as fond of a game as they are of a fight,
    My Paw said so.
An' all of the animals found in the wood
Ain't always ferocious. Most times they are good.

The trouble is mostly they're misunderstood,
    My Paw said so.
You can think what you like, but I stick to it when
    My Paw said so.
An' I'll keep right on sayin,' again an' again,
    My Paw said so.
Maybe foxes don't talk to such people as you,
An' bears never show you the tricks they can do,
But I know that the stories I'm tellin' are true,
    My Paw said so.

——Edgar Guest

Left: Through the falling leaves and over the fence, we see the village of Hightown, Virginia—on US Highway 250. *Above:* Kneeling in the autumn leaves, a father shares the wonders of the Kentucky landscape with his son. He remembers the time when, as a boy, he came to this same spot with his own father and heard the stories of their ancestors coming west with Daniel Boone to build a new life in these untamed, yet promising hills.

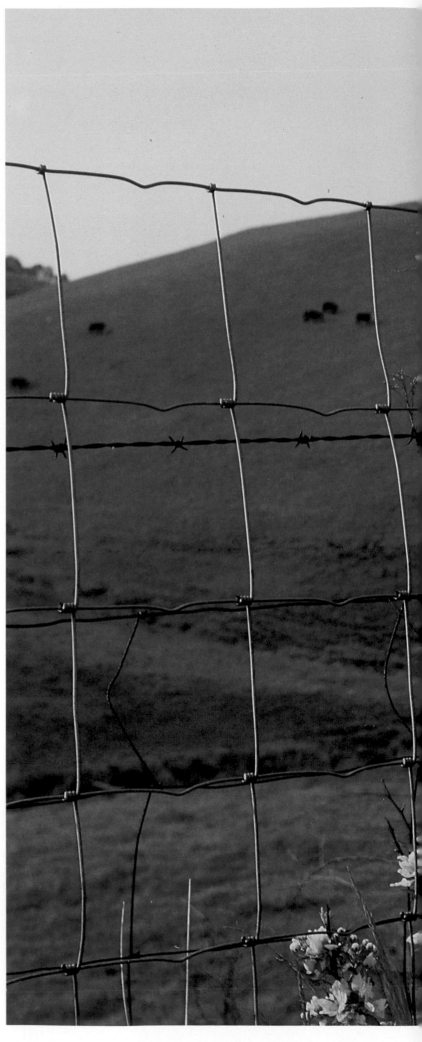

NATURE'S PLAY

Blue is the sky dome over the green,
Golden the sunshine sifting between
Branches that lazily sway in the breeze,
Showering the shadows under the trees
With arrows of light from the quiver of noon,
By the bow whose arch is the bright sky of June.

Sweet is the air with the perfume of flowers
Yielding their life through the long sunny hours;
With the song of the birds and the kiss of the dawn
To give them a welcome, their beauty was born.
And now seeks the sun its nightly repose,
While over its couch drapes a curtain of rose.

The clouds rolling upward in waves from the west,
Wear the colors of heaven with silvery crest,
Where the moon proudly sailing disperses her light
Till the little stars modestly creep out of sight.
These beautiful charms of the night and the day
Are glorious acts in Nature's grand play.

——*Benj F Brown*

Above: An Amish family takes a horsedrawn outing in the fertile Shenandoah Valley—both part of Virginia's wonderful heritage. *Right:* Cattle graze and flowers climb a fence in the lushness of southwestern Virginia.

THOUGHTS IN AUTUMN

Yes, thou art welcome, Autumn! all thy changes,
    From fitful gloom, to sunny skies serene,
The starry vaults, o'er which the charmed eye ranges,
    And cold, clear moonlight, touching every scene
With a peculiar sadness, are sweet things,
To which my heart congenial fondly clings.

There is a moral in the withered wreaths
    And faded garlands that adorn thy bowers;
Each blighted shrub, chilled flower, or seared leaf breathes
    Of parted days, and brighter by-gone hours,
Contrasting with the present dreary scene
Spring's budding beauties, pleasures which have been.

                              ——*Anna Peyre Dinnies*

Above: It's harvest time on the tobacco farms of Tennessee. *Right:* This long road home leads through the hills and dales of southwestern Virginia.

SOLITUDE

The ceaseless hum of men, the dusty streets
  Crowded with multitudinous life; the din
  Of toil and traffic, and the woe and sin,
The dweller in the populous city meets:
These have I left to seek the cool retreats
  Of the untrodden forest, where, in bowers
  Builded by Nature's hand, inlaid with flowers,
And roofed with ivy, on the mossy seats
  Reclining, I can while away the hours
In sweetest converse with old books, or give
My thoughts to God; or fancies fugitive
  Indulge, while over me their radiant showers
Of rarest blossoms the old trees shake down,
And thanks to Him my meditations crown!

——*William H Burleigh*

Left: A tidal stream winds its way amid the dunes to the Atlantic Ocean, on Georgia's Jekyll Island, near St Andrew's Sound.

LEAVING HOME

Within an ivied mountain porch a vase
   Is filled with bleeding hearts, o'er which is hung
   The portrait of a man when he was young—
A sabered scion of a fighting race.
A dog is peering in his master's face—
   That of an only son, who, called among
   His country's saviors, stands with stifled tongue
Before his mother in a fond embrace.

The mother's mother, fearing sacrifice,
   Looks strangely at the stars and stripes afloat;
To hide the moisture welling in his eyes,
   The waiting father turns to brush his coat,
While sister fumbles at her dress and tries
   To gulp the gorge arising in her throat.

———*Willis Hudspeth*

This old road *(left)* winds toward a Tennessee mountaintop under a canopy of brilliant autumn leaves—which in times past, and no doubt in 'times future,' has served to conceal many a 'white lightning' still, and has called many a country boy back home from the city.

Above: A tree bursts into fall foliage on this classic modern Tennessee homestead. The '57 Chevy reminds one of *Thunder Road*—the restless postwar youth of the fifties, homebuilt hotrods and a quiet country landscape that blazed with, and somehow encouraged, feats of untamed derring-do.

THE OLD LOG HOUSE THAT
GRANDPA BUILT

The old log house that grandpa built
Is standing where the fairies spilt
The seeds of peaches, tupelos,
Persimmons, firs and mistletoes.

The plaster lingers in the chinks;
Although the ridgepiece slightly sinks,
The cobbled chimney points as true
As in the days of sixty-two.

The absent attic boards reveal
The spokes in grandma's spinning wheel;
White clematis is vining still
Outside the kitchen window sill.

An iron pump is fastened where
The curving sweep and bucket were;
A platform with a mortared ledge
Supplants the soft and mossy edge.

Down by the river path is heard
Familiar musings of a bird,
And as I pass a honey hive
Endearing memories revive.

Meandering amid the glint,
I crush a stalk of peppermint
Declining in the garden yard,
And something makes me swallow hard.

Among the southern mansions which
Survive the ante-bellum rich,
Not one outvies, though trimmed with gilt,
The old log house that grandpa built.

——*Willis Hudspeth*

Above: Grandpa and his cronies enjoy a Veteran's Day celebration, Southern-style. Veterans all, they proudly salute the stars and stripes, although in his heart, Grandpa is still partial to the stars and bars.

Right: Grandpa's old house that has long since stood the test of time, weathers yet another southern autumn; getting set in its timbers once again for the chill and damp of winter.

Like their parents and grandparents on the clear summer morns of bygone years, these children romp through a Shenandoah Valley pasture.

THE GREAT

LAKES

from

MY NATIVE VILLAGE

There lies a village in a peaceful vale,
  With sloping hills and waving woods around,
Fenced from the blasts. There never ruder gale
  Bows the tall grass that covers all the ground;
And planted shrubs are there, and cherished
flowers,
And a bright verdure, born of gentler showers.

'Twas there my young existence was begun,
  My earliest sports were on its flowery green,
And often, when my schoolboy task was done,
  I climbed its hills to view the pleasant scene,
And stood and gazed till the sun's setting ray
Shone on the height, the sweetest of the day.

There, when that hour of mellow light was come,
  And mountain shadows cooled the ripened grain,
I watched the weary yeoman plodding home,
  In the lone path that winds across the plain,
To rest his limbs, and watch his child at play,
And tell him o'er the labours of the day.

And when the woods put on their autumn glow,
  And the bright sun came in among the trees,
And leaves were gathering in the glen below,
  Swept softly from the mountains by the breeze,
I wandered till the starlight on the stream
At length awoke me from my fairy dream.

Ah! happy days, too happy to return,
  Fled on the wings of youth's departed years,
A bitter lesson has been mine to learn,
  The truth of life, its labours, pains, and fears;
Yet does the memory of my boyhood stay,
A twilight of the brightness passed away.

My thoughts steal back to that sweet village still,
  Its flowers and peaceful shades before me rise;
The play-place, and the prospect from the hill,
  Its summer verdure, and autumnal dyes;
The present brings its storms; but, while they last,
I shelter me in the delightful past.

——*John H Bryant*

Previous spread: The Michigan shore of one of those great lakes which were once known as 'The Great Inland Seas.' *Above:* Like a village somewhere in Sweden, this pristine view of Center City, Minnesota seems to emanate fresh northern air.

Right: As this apple vendor of Swedish descent offers his wares, he actually appears to glow from within—or is it the small-town sunshine of Frontenac, Minnesota?

OCTOBER DAYS

In the golden haze of October days,
   In the woodland valleys and hills
There are showers of gold for the leaves grown old,
   Drop fast into Nature's tills.

Then the prickly burrs, when the sharp wind stirs
   Every branch of the chestnut tree,
Opened wide by frost, never heed the cost,
   But give of their treasures free.

O those woodland hills, how their beauty thrills,
   Bright tinted from red to gold;
'Tis a farewell song while we drift along
   Toward the days when the year is old.

————*Benj F Brown*

Left: A leaf-strewn two lane blacktop is a sign of impending winter—'mitten weather'—in the woods of rural Michigan. This old barn *(above)* affords an aged viewpoint for these very charming farm folk. Inadvertent windows and October's aromatic straw are but a few of the riches contained in the barns of Wisconsin, 'America's Dairyland.' *Overleaf:* Soon, with the winter's snows, some Michiganders will have to find another route to their favorite secluded spot, as the old dirt road is already in the depths of autumn.

from

AMERICAN WINTER

'Tis then the time from hoarding cribs to feed
The ox laborious, and the noble steed;
'Tis then the time to tend the bleating fold,
To strew with litter, and to fence from cold.
The cattle fed, the fuel piled within,
At setting day the blissful hours begin;
'Tis then, sole owner of his little cot,
The farmer feels his independent lot;
Hears, with the crackling blaze that lights the wall,
The voice of gladness and of nature call;
Beholds his children play, their mother smile,
And tastes with them the fruit of summer's toil.

From stormy heavens the mantling clouds unrolled,
The sky is bright, the air serenely cold.
The keen northwest, that heaps the drifted snows,
For months entire o'er frozen regions blows;
Man braves his blast; his gelid breath inhales,
And feels more vigorous as the frost prevails.

——*David Humphreys*

'The horse knows the way to carry the sleigh' sing these happy Wisconsin folks off on sleigh ride together *(left)*—an activity much favored during the long northern winter. There are much worse ways to spend a winter evening than 'snug and cozy' before the crackling fire of this Minnesota resort cabin *(above)*.

SPRINGTIME

In the shade of the old garden apple tree resting;
    While breezes play softly 'mid blossoms and leaves,
And in its green branches the robins are nesting;
    Glad notes of the springtime my fancy receives.
A perfume delicious my breath is inhaling,
    The arch of the sky wears a lovely May blue,
And over its sea the white clouds are sailing,
    Till, harbored in sunlight, they vanish from view.

Now down by the meadows where flowers are springing,
    The swallows are curving in crescents of light,
While sweet on the air falls the jubilant singing
    Of birds new redeemed from the winter's long night.
O, glorious springtime, when earth is awaking,
    And Nature in beautiful garments is dressed;
Thy smile giveth life to each day's undertaking,
    Thy generous heart ever brings us the best.

——*Benj F Brown*

Fruit trees begin to blossom and these girls *(left)* enjoy the spring days before summer, and 'green apple bellyache time' in Michigan. *Above:* This Wisconsin barn is painted with a mural depicting the three physical planes—air, sea and land—in a paean to life on Earth. *Right:* These wild blackeyed Susans border a farm field near Black River Falls, in Jackson County, Wisconsin. *Overleaf:* In the time-honored tradition of rural mercantilism, this country store offers 'your' goods for all purposes in Bosstown, Wisconsin.

AUTUMN EVENING

Behold the western evening light!
  It melts in deepening gloom;
So calmly Christians sink away,
  Descending to the tomb.

The wind breathes low; the withering leaf
  Scarce whispers from the tree;
So gently flows the parting breath,
  When good men cease to be.

How beautiful on all the hills
  The crimson light is shed!
'Tis like the peace the Christian gives
  To mourners round his bed.

How mildly on the wandering cloud
  The sunset beam is cast!
'Tis like the memory left behind
  When loved ones breathe their last.

And now, above the dews of night,
  The yellow star appears;
So faith springs in the heart of those
  Whose eyes are bathed in tears.

But soon the morning's happier light
  Its glory shall restore;
And eyelids that are sealed in death
  Shall wake, to close no more.

——*W B O Peabody*

Above: A Michigan sunset view reminds us that almost any lake can be 'great.' Though Lake Michigan is second in size among the Great Lakes, it is second to none in terms of 'greatness.'

Right: The fall foliage cloaks this narrow road through the Wisconsin woods, as occasional patches of sunlight dapple on the berm. Maples, poplars and other trees of the misleadingly named 'scrub woods' combine to weave this delicate tapestry.

from
A HARVEST MASQUERADE

The passing menace of the clouds
revealed
A slender sickle in the starry field,
Illumining the fodder shocks that stood
Like Indian tents against the river wood.

Exploding softly in the early night,
A fountain dropped its jets of golden light,
And glittered only long enough to be
Transformed to meteoric nebulae.

This was the signal for a bursting shout
From young and older settlers starting out
In constellation dress and countenance
To decorate a neighbor's harvest dance.

The smiling pumpkins, lighted for the fete,
With gourd-made lanterns raised above the gate,
In keeping with the heavens, picturesque,
Shone forth a welcome equally grotesque.

——*Willis Hudspeth*

Left: These shocks of grain husks seem like monuments to the harvest—lit by the fading sun, watched over by the early moon. *Overleaf:* Like Abe Lincoln, this Illinois road follows the 'straight and narrow'—through the the winter landscape.

THE GREAT

PLAINS

A GRASSLAND FARMSTEAD

Where buffaloes once pawed their prairie trails,
   The loaded coaches of a train commence
   This picture of the great munificence
Of progress in the west which now prevails.
The puffing locomotive almost fails;
   The cars are wriggling up the eminence,
   Jar forcibly the viaduct and fence,
And lengthen out along the level rails.

Deep drifts of snow have melted in the run:
   An iron windmill pumps a constant flow,
But palpitates too speedily for one
   Inclining to the vagrant while ago,
Who, having climbed the red caboose, is done
   With places where he has to plow and sow.

———*Willis Hudspeth*

Previous page: This cattle drive along US Route 83 in South Dakota, gives an ink-ling of what 'life is about' in the Great Plains states, 'Where seldom is heard a dis-couraging word, and the sky is not cloudy all day.' *Above:* This South Dakotan farmer seems to think that his hard work is well worth it, and perhaps even a city slicker might be tempted to the difficult agricultural life by a pristine farmstead such as this *(right)*, with a yellow windmill rising above it like a welcoming beacon.

Wagons, buckboards and 'prairie schooners' on exhibit at the historic trail town of Cody, Wyoming *(below)* remind us of highways of yesterday—when the Oregon Trail and the old Bozeman Trail led immigrants westward through unimaginable difficulty; and oxen, mules and horses brought families west on the 'Interstates' of the Western Frontier—which were comprised of little more than two ruts across a vast and nearly impassable wilderness.

THE DEVIL'S HEAD

Near that gigantic column, Chimney Rock,
   Distending from the burning under bed,
   A graven profile of the devil's head
Sticks outward frowardly in lines that mock.
The first impression is a subtle shock;
   The creek rolls like a mass of molten lead,
   And croaking vultures amplify the dread
Careening from the timber in a flock.

For months no rain has fallen from the sky—
   The first occurrence of the kind for years;
The foliage is turning brown and dry.
   A superstitious guide betrays his fears
That this strange image has an evil eye
   And brought the scourge upon the mountaineers.

——*Willis Hudspeth*

Left: Shown here is the Wind River Canyon, with US Route 26 running beside the river, in west central Wyoming. Wyoming's Wind River Range—a spur of the Rocky Mountains—is located nearby.

Above: This old cabin faces the ancient granite monadnock, Devil's Tower—located in Wyoming near the Fourche River. Devil's Tower National Monument is due west, on the Little Missouri River.

A PRAIRIE REVERIE

Where have I heard that pastoral before?
   Oh, yes, out in the valley where a snipe
   Is playing something like a shepherd's pipe—
Out where the river joins a reedy moor.
How often, roughing on the range, that score
   Has gripped me in its solitary gripe
   About the time the rye and oats were ripe!
It takes me loping to the years of yore.

Please play that reverie again for me;
   It makes me see the spotted yearlings browse,
As in the heedless days of eighty-three.
   I love to hear that piping while I drowse,
To sense the wide and wild serenity,
   And listen to the mooing of the cows.

            ——*Willis Hudspeth*

Above: Plying the fields with his combine, this farmer is a man alone on the flat-lands, quite apart from the rancher, whose herds and comrades keep him company. *Left:* These cowhands give their hard-working steeds a rest, and take time to spin a yarn or two.

Below right: Center stage at Cheyenne, Wyoming's Frontier Days celebration. Mingled with the American flags being carried by these modern day Annie Oakleys, there are left to right: the Cheyenne Frontier Days commemorative flag; the Wyoming state flag; the Colorado state flag; the Canadian national flag; the British Columbia provincial flag; the National Rodeo Cowboy Association flag; and a flag celebrating the Arabian horse—a breed which brought speed and strength to Western horsemanship: the bearer of this flag is seated upon an Arabian.

THE SOUTHWEST

Below: US Route 50 against a backdrop of one of Nevada's impressive mountain ranges. Route 50 traverses the middle of the state—from California on through Utah.

RAINBOW BRIDGE

A wide, precipitous and trackless wild,
   Impassable by vehicle or ass,
     Where rocks, rocks, rocks are jungled in a mass;
Rocks—massive, little, scattered, leaning, piled;
Rocks—dirty, splintered, rough and smoothly tiled,
   In thorny chaparral and rusty grass;
     Rocks—bright and clean, too different to class,
One-colored, mottled, striped, clear and riled.

Above this lonely gorgeous setting bows
   The famous red and yellow sandstone arc
Across a rapid rivulet that flows
   From Navaho and zigzags through the park.
When Nature built it not an Indian knows,
   And nowhere is an explicating mark.

——Willis Hudspeth

Only at one point in the continental United States do the boundary lines of four states—Utah, Colorado, New Mexico and Arizona—come together; the 'Four Corners' area, just a few miles west of Monument Valley, where these Navajo boys *(left)* shepherd their sheep.

Accessible by US Highway 163, Monument Valley Navajo Tribal Park is part of the extensive Navajo Indian Reservation, which extends into Utah and Arizona, and of course encompasses Monument Valley itself—scene of many a sensational sunset display of contrasts *(above)*.

AN OLD MISSION

Erected by a roving Spanish band,
   Its walls, adobe, crumbling, represent
   An aged missionary, gray and bent,
Who waits migration to a better land.
A yucca bristles by a path of sand,
   Wherein the rambler stumbled to repent
   Of wasted life, or to, perchance, lament
A weakness under which he could not stand.

A climbing vine has reached the roofless eaves,
   And clings upon the edifice of clay;
A tropic wind has singed the curling leaves
   Unable longer to pursue their way.
It seems the spirit of the picture grieves
   O'er dissolution which no man can stay.

——*Willis Hudspeth*

Left: A narrow country road winds through Canyon de Chelly, near Chinle, Arizona—so near to, yet so very, very far from US Route 191. Settled in Prehistoric times by the long-gone Anasazi civilization, Canyon de Chelly is today off-limits to anyone without the expressed permission of the Navajo tribal leadership. The Painted Cliffs, near New Mexico's western border, form a backdrop to this mission church *(above)* along old US Route 66.

Below: Despite a lot of popular mythologizing about Texas being 'a widely diversified state, producing everything from gypsum to peaches,' Texas is comprised mainly of *cattle, cowboys* and *oil wells*. And, about those cattle, well '... their eyes are blazin' fire and their hooves are made of steel ....'

A TWIG OF SAGEBRUSH

For miles and miles the desert widens through
   That region of the Red Man's broken bow,
   Where white-caps, indistinct and row on row,
Make notches in the long horizon's blue.
Vast rolling areas of sage-green hue
   Expand as far as arid Idaho,
   And, interspersed, the thorny cacti blow
A dainty coloration in the view.

With broad-brimmed hat and swinging pistol sheath,
   The cowboy leaps his steed of tossing mane;
While rounding up the cattle on the heath,
   Or on the steeps, he draws a careful rein,
But gallops in abandon from the wreath
   Of dust he makes upon the sunny plain.

——*Willis Hudspeth*

WINDS OF TEXAS

The wolf-howl of the winds of Texas sweeps through the wide
    and aching night:
From the Gulf, salty, sea-scented,
Rising, lifting over the wet white wings of Galveston,
Dipping to the Alamo, chiming, swinging with the mission bells
    in their towers,
Pouring through Austin, pink-domed among its river-carved
    hills;
Sounding its bragging horns of bravado to the railroad-vaunting
    cities, to their lit windows lifted high in its air-track;
Feeling out the cotton blooms, combing the young corn,
Calling to the cattle as they browse;
Singing with mighty gusto to the ranchman in his shack under
    the cliff,
Loping out for the big spaces,
Howling for hunger and thirst of deep desire;
Answering the call of the moon, driving the balloon-sailed
    clouds,
Searching the sky, pricking eager ears for the footsteps of the
    sun on the plains,
Shouting for joy of shaking out the stillness from wide and lofty
    spaces;
Calling, calling,
Leaping, loping,
Roaring fiercely onward,
The wolf-howl of the winds of Texas sweeps through the wide
    and aching night.

——Harriet Monroe

Originally a large rut formed by one of Pecos Bill's bootheels when he tried to dis-
mount *exactly* at the time his horse smelled water, this old blacktop *(left)* winds
through the Davis Mountains of western Texas heading for the Rio Grande. Near
Fort Worth, drovers work a herd of rangy longhorns *(above)* on the Westfork cattle
ranch. *Overleaf:* This aerial photo of an East Texas farm shows the spare fertility
of the land. East Texas claims to produce general cash crops, including grains, fruit
and cotton—but we know that that 'house' is really a temporary shelter for longhorns. Texans rarely venture indoors, except to fetch barbeque sauce.

THE MOUNTAIN

WEST

ODE OF A MOUNTAINEER

I think the city stores are grand,
   With polish, heat and fume;
But I am longing for the land
   Of sunshine, air and room.
The pines and canyons call me back
To life around my mountain shack.

I have enjoyed the limousines,
   Soft-cushioned, for a time;
But I am sighing for the scenes
   Where I shall have to climb,
Or hold fast in the old stage-hack
That jostles past my mountain shack.

I like the pavements, level, straight,
   Without a gulch or bluff;
But I am starting for the state
   Whose roads are steep and rough,
Up to whose jagged peaks a track
Leads winding from my mountain shack.

——*Willis Hudspeth*

Previous page: Going-to-the-Sun Highway in Glacier National Park leads us up toward the Continental Divide, in western Montana. Pack trips such as this one *(left)*—through Montana's beautiful, mountainous Pintler Peak country are always memorable occasions. *Above:* Spanning three generations of Montanans, an old cowboy poses with his granddaughter against a verdant backdrop.

from
LINES WRITTEN ON THE ROCKY MOUNTAINS

These mountains, piercing the blue sky
    With their eternal cones of ice;
The torrents dashing from on high,
    O'er rock and crag and precipice;
Change not, but still remain as ever,
    Unwasting, deathless, and sublime,
And will remain while lightnings quiver,
    Or stars the hoary summits climb,
Or rolls the thunder-chariot of eternal Time.

It is not so with all—I change,
    And waste as with a living death,
Like one that hath become a strange,
    Unwelcome guest, and lingereth
Among the memories of the past,
    Where he is a forgotten name;
For Time hath greater power to blast
    The hopes, the feelings, and the fame,
To make the passions fierce, or their first
strength to tame.

Perhaps, when I have passed away,
    Like the sad echo of a dream,
There may be some one found to say
    A word that might like sorrow seem.
That I would have—one saddened tear,
    One kindly and regretting thought—
Grant me but that!—and even here,
    Here, in this lone, unpeopled spot,
To breathe away this life of pain, I murmur not.

——*Albert Pike*

Above: On its way to 'the sweet bye and bye,' a rainbow rises through the air over Cache Valley, Utah. *Right:* This is a view of Heaven's Peak, as seen from Going-to-the-Sun Highway, in Glacier National Park, Montana. If you step back a bit, and let your focus widen, you may be able to glimpse the gigantic halo surrounding the mountain.

THE HOME-TOWN

Some folks leave home for money
And some leave home for fame,
Some seek skies always sunny,
And some depart in shame.
I care not what the reason
Men travel east or west,
Or what the month or season—
The home-town is the best.

The home-town is the glad town
Where something real abides;
'Tis not the money-mad town
That all its spirit hides.
Though strangers scoff and flout it
And even jeer its name,
It has a charm about it
No other town can claim.

The home-town skies seem bluer
Than skies that stretch away.
The home-town friends seem truer
And kinder through the day;
And whether glum or cheery
Light-hearted or depressed,
Or struggle-fit or weary,
I like the home-town best.

Let him who will, go wander
To distant towns to live,
Of some things I am fonder
Than all they have to give.
The gold of distant places
Could not repay me quite
For those familiar faces
That keep the home-town bright.

——*Edgar Guest*

Beyond the picturesque little town of West Glacier, Montana *(above)* is the west entrance of Glacier National Park, and the beginning of Going-to-the--Sun Highway, which connects at either end to US Route 2, and winds across the park.

Accessible by the Going-to-the-Sun Highway, Lake McDonald Lodge *(right)*, overlooking the lake, was originally part of a network of lodges built by the Great Northern Railroad as a spur to the development of tourism in Glacier National Park itself.

THE ROCKY ROUTE

The strait and narrow way is not
  A beaten path to gold.
It passes through a lonely spot
  Of failures manifold,
Most difficult to penetrate;
But, oh, the exercise is great!

You lovers of artistic deeps
  With eagerness to scout
And sketch among the rugged steeps,
  Look up the Rocky Route.
Upon a boulder you may land;
But, oh, the scenery is grand!

And all of you who want to teach
  The people what is best—
Especially you who would preach
  From individual test—
You may be sidetracked on this line;
But, oh, the inspiration's fine!

——*Willis Hudspeth*

Left: A young photographer prepares to truly take a 'closeup' shot of some mountain sheep near the ice fields on Columbia Mountain in west central Alberta. *Above:* Wildflowers bloom beside a hillside path in marvellous Glacier National Park, Montana.

Twisting, turning US Route 212 passes near Pilot Peak *(below)* in the Absaroka Range of the Rocky Mountains. This rugged, handsome landscape lies a few miles southeast of Cook City, Montana—just over the Wyoming border.

from
TOO HIGH

Where ridges rise up through the clouds,
And awe-inspiring art enshrouds
The master canyons' craggy walls;
Where gurgle white the waterfalls
From melting, ice-appareled peaks
To placid-running valley creeks,
I found a trail of recreation
That led to healthful meditation.

A marvel of the continent—
A Rocky Mountain monument—
Reflected vigor in each crest,
Associating thoughts of rest
With chiseled gardens of the gods,
Wherein the Sculptor threw the odds

And ends of grandeur that were left,
It seemed,
   When these great hills were cleft.

Its apex reaching to the sky,
A mighty summit towered nigh;
Secure, exalted and serene,
It pointed to the golden mean,
Directing undiscerning man
Up to the higher, wiser plan—
Up where, among the active spheres,
Fatigue in balance disappears.

Inspired by these environments
Of majesty and reverence,

I started up the steepest cone
That pinnacled the range—alone.
I followed in the ferny aisles,
Rewound around the sheer defiles,
And, after many hours of hope,
I tarried half way up the slope.

Jack-in-the-pulpits mutely preached
Of restfulness that may be reached
Around the lighted altar fires
Of sheltered tarns and granite spires,
Where, in the frankincense and myrrh
Exuding from the juniper,
The golden-vested songsters sing
Their sweet processionals of spring.

——*Willis Hudspeth*

Left: A pack string fords a stream near the base of Pendergraft Peak in Wyoming's Grand Teton National Park, near the Idaho border. In times past, these folks might have been miners prospecting for ore. These days, pack trains may be those of hunters or campers.

Above: This is a photograph of the Medicine Bow Peak area, part of the Eastern Rockies, in southeastern Wyoming. 'Medicine Bow,' like many other North (and South) American place names, is the invention of the area's original inhabitants—the various American Indian tribes.

FISHING

My grandfather said with a toss of his head,
    As he sat at the fire making flies,
Tying silk upon hooks for his old leather books
    And being mighty proud of his ties:
'Oh, the sport is a joy! But remember, my boy,
    Only hungry men work for the dish.
The creel's but a part of this glorious art;
    There is much more to fishing than fish.

'From spring unto fall I can answer the call
    To go out on my favorite streams,
And when wintry winds bite I can sit here at night,
    Enjoying my fancies and dreams.
For the soul can be stirred, both by blossom and bird,
    And the wonders that lie all about.
There are volumes of lore it's a joy to explore;
    Oh, there's much more to fishing than trout.

'It's not all in the catch; there's a thrill in the hatch,
    And knowing the birds by their song.
There's the tying of hooks and the reading of books,
    Which last a man all his life long;
Not a fisherman he who contented can be
    With the whirr of the reel and the swish
Of a taut running line, for the art is too fine!
    There is much more to fishing than fish.'

——*Edgar Guest*

Left: Pelican Creek, a fishing ground where many a 'big one' has 'managed to slip from the hook' after 'hours of battle,' winds toward the eastern boundary *(at rear)* of Yellowstone National Park, Wyoming. *Above:* This young angler has caught a trout—beginner's luck, no doubt—in Prince Albert National Park in central Saskatchewan, near Provincial Highway 2.

from
TOO HIGH

Above the elevated view
Was spread the bright celestial blue
That rolls the artist's eye and swells
His vision with ecstatic spells,
Till, dreaming in the tranquil breeze
And scenting balsam from the trees,
He loses in the arid haze
Off on the plains his ardent gaze.

Beyond a cabin by a pine,
Advancing to the timber line,
Where vegetation stunts and dies
And banks of snow increase in size,
I clambered through the wintry blast
Until the top was gained at last—
The farthest tip of earthly goal.
The scene disquieted my soul.

I saw the entrance of a chasm
Yawn wide as in a hunger spasm;
Down in the cold, abysmal black
I, cautious, peeped and startled back.

——*Willis Hudspeth*

Above: A traveller stands at the summit of Bear Tooth Pass, on US Highway 212 near the Montana/Wyoming border, in Custer National Forest. In the northern Great Plains states, one can stop the car almost anywhere, and just looking around, one can find a striking vista, such as that from Bear Tooth Pass *(right)*. Camping out on a shoreline always seems 'something extra,' especially in locales such as Cooks Lake *(overleaf),* in Wyoming's Bridger Wilderness Area.

Below: The beauties of a cloud-mottled day reflect in depthless Lake Tahoe. A dying tree catches the sunlight as if in farewell to its fellows, in shadow. The quiet and serenity evidenced here belies the extreme popularity of this—and the entire Sierra Nevada—area.

A MOUNTAIN LAKE

Beyond the grandeurs of the wide plateau,
    Against a Rocky Mountain's timber line,
    Surrounded by a frame of straggling pine,
A picture hangs in Colorado's show.
My pencils tipped with inspiration's glow,
    I try to reproduce the lucent shrine—
    The cleft, the granite boulders and the mine,
The mirrored zenith and the peak of snow.

I strive to draw the shimmer in the sheen,
    The balmy dank, the soundless unrestraint,
A lone parnassia bowing in the scene.
    My colors are, alas, too marked or faint.
And yet these lines suggest, I fondly ween,
    The exaltation which I cannot paint.

——*Willis Hudspeth*

CARE-FREE YOUTH

The skies are blue and the sun is out and the
    grass is green and soft
And the old charm's back in the apple tree
    and it calls a boy aloft;
And the same low voice that the old don't hear,
    but the care-free youngsters do,
Is calling them to the fields and streams and
    the joys that once I knew.
And if youth be wild desire for play and care
    is the mark of men,
Beneath the skin that Time has tanned I'm a
    madcap youngster then.

Far richer than king with his crown of gold and
    his heavy weight of care
Is the sunburned boy with his stone-bruised feet
    and his tousled shock of hair;
For the king can hear but the cry of hate or the
    sickly sound of praise,
And lost to him are the voices sweet that called
    in his boyhood days.
Far better than ruler, with pomp and power
    and riches, is it to be
The urchin gay in his tattered clothes that is
    climbing the apple tree.

Oh, once I heard all the calls that come to the
    quick, glad ears of boys,
And a certain spot on the river bank told me of
    its many joys,
And certain fields and certain trees were loyal
    friends to me,
And I knew the birds, and I owned a dog, and
    we both could hear and see.
Oh, never from tongues of men have dropped
    such messages wholly glad
As the things that live in the great outdoors
    once told to a little lad.

And I'm sorry for him who cannot hear what
    the tall trees have to say,
Who is deaf to the call of a running stream
    and the lanes that lead to play.
The boy that shins up the faithful elm or
    sprawls on a river bank
Is more richly blessed with the joys of life than
    any old man of rank.
For youth is the golden time of life, and this
    battered old heart of mine
Beats fast to the march of its old-time joys,
    when the sun begins to shine.

——*Edgar Guest*

At left, a young participant in an Eastern European ethnic festival at Yegreville, Alberta, honors his immigrant ancestors. Even the North American immigrant influxes of the 19th and 20th centuries failed to truly penetrate Canada's vast natural abundance and pure, native beauty—no wonder that Canadians love to celebrate!

With abundant and often spectacular Rocky Mountain vistas, and marvellous coastal scenery, the appellation 'Beautiful' is an apt provincial motto for British Columbia, where this pond *(above)* provides pause for reflection, with the Canadian coastal mountains in the background.

THE SCHOOLHOUSE
ON THE HILL

In the golden summer morning,
   Down the sunny winding road,
By the verdant, flowery meadows;
   How my heart with joy o'erflowed—
O, the happy days of childhood,
   Recollection brings a thrill,
As in fancy now I wander
   Near the schoolhouse on the hill.

Birds are singing by the wayside,
   There's a nest 'mid bowers of green,
Berries ripe stain little fingers
   While they search the briars between;
Wealth of beauty, joy and sunshine,
   Nature's best our longings fill
While we trudge along the pathway
   Towards the schoolhouse on the hill.

Blue the skies that shine above it,
   Curtained by the whispering trees,
Rich the memories clustering round it,
   Sweeter than the summer breeze.
Smooth and hollow is its doorstep,
   Worn and thin its ancient sill
By the little feet that entered
   In the schoolhouse on the hill.

——Benj F Brown

This abandoned schoolhouse is located near Summer Lake, in south central Oregon, 'just off' State Route 31. Many children have passed through its doors, and no doubt, some who have left for 'faraway places' remember this old white building with fond recollections of their own, seemingly faraway, youth.

Below: An old abandoned cabin continues its stand, alone with its memories, on the plains, with the Tetons looming in the background—just next door to Yellowstone National Park, in northwest Wyoming.

A SOD HOUSE

Surviving by a level prairie way
   That parallels a swamp of wind-swept reeds,
   Its layered roofing streaked with grass and weeds,
A sod house settles in a vale of hay.
One side, which leans, is strengthened with a stay;
   Thick-walled and weather-worn, the entrance needs
   New chinking, and the vestibule that leads
Back in the cave is sagging from decay.

The wooden pump and trough are cracked and dry;
   A one-horse rake is rusting in the view;
Some logs and saplings in the stable lie
   Where half the musty top has fallen through,
And blowing tumble-weeds are stacking high
   Where cantaloupes and watermelons grew.

——*Willis Hudspeth*

THE FAR NORTH

from

THE SHOOTING OF DAN McGREW

A bunch of the boys were whooping it up in the Malamute
saloon;
The kid that handles the music-box was hitting a jag-time tune;
Back of the bar, in a solo game, sat Dangerous Dan McGrew,
And watching his luck was his light-of-love, the lady that's
known as Lou.

When out of the night, which was fifty below, and into the din
and the glare,
There stumbled a miner fresh from the creeks, dog-dirty, and
loaded for bear.
He looked like a man with a foot in the grave and scarcely the
strength of a louse,
Yet he tilted a poke of dust on the bar, and he called for drinks
for the house.
There was none could place the stranger's face, though we
searched ourselves for a clue;
But we drank his health, and the last to drink was Dangerous
Dan McGrew.

Then on a sudden the music changed, so soft that you scarce
could hear;
But you felt that your life had been looted clean of all that it
once held dear;
That someone had stolen the woman you loved; that her love
was a devil's lie;
That your guts were gone, and the best for you was to crawl
away and die.
'Twas the crowning cry of a heart's despair, and it thrilled you
through and through—
'I guess I'll make it a spread misere,' said Dangerous Dan
McGrew.

Then I ducked my head, and the lights went out, and two guns
blazed in the dark,
And a woman screamed, and the lights went up, and two men
lay stiff and stark.
Pitched on his head, and pumped full of lead, was Dangerous
Dan McGrew,
While the man from the creeks lay clutched to the breast of the
lady that's known as Lou.

These are the simple facts of the case, and I guess I ought to
know.
They say that the stranger was crazed with 'hooch,' and I'm
not denying it's so.
I'm not so wise as the lawyer guys, but strictly between us
two—
The woman that kissed him and—pinched his poke—was the
lady that's known as Lou.

——*Robert Service*

Previous page: Beneath the midnight sun where country roads are defined by
dogsleds and sealskin kayaks, these men stand on Lee Point, Ellesmere Island—
largest of the Elizabeth Islands, part of Canada's Northwest Territories, in the Arctic
Ocean. Afognak Island lies just north of Kodiak Island, near Cook Inlet in the Gulf
of Alaska. *Right:* Summer in Canada's Northwest Territories can be quite warm, as
witnessed by this canoeist (who, by the way is not named 'Lou,' despite any expecta-
tions) on the Nahanni River, which flows out of the MacKenzie Mountains and ul-
timately into the MacKenzie River. Mount Wilson—not to be confused with the
eponymous mountain in southern California—rises before her.

from

THE SPELL OF THE YUKON

There's a land where the mountains are nameless,
    And the rivers all run God knows where;
There are lives that are erring and aimless,
    And deaths that just hang by a hair;
There are hardships that nobody reckons;
    There are valleys unpeopled and still;
There's a land—oh, it beckons and beckons,
    And I want to go back—and I will.

There's gold, and it's haunting and haunting;
    It's luring me on as of old;
Yet it isn't the gold that I'm wanting
    So much as just finding the gold.
It's the great, big, broad land 'way up yonder,
    It's the forests where silence has lease;
It's the beauty that thrills me with wonder,
    It's the stillness that fills me with peace.

——Robert Service

Above: These backwoods packers repose briefly, with a paddle and a set of caribou antlers on the shore of Baker Lake, in Canada's Northwest Territories. Bush pilots are important suppliers for expeditions in the far north. *At right,* an oil drum and other equipment is unloaded on the banks of the Firth River in Alaska's Yukon territory. *Below:* Among the deep forests of the Yukon's headwaters, the ancient cabin of an old sourdough prospector slowly accumulates an insulating roof layer of moss—very much appreciated, come the Alaskan wintertime.

from

THE HEART OF THE SOURDOUGH

There where the mighty mountains bare their
  fangs unto the moon,
There where the sullen sun-dogs glare in the
  snow-bright, bitter noon,
And the glacier-glutted streams sweep down at
  the clarion call of June.

There where the livid tundras keep their tryst
  with the tranquil snows;
There where the silences are spawned, and the
  light of hell-fire flows
Into the bowl of the midnight sky, violet, amber
  and rose.

——*Robert Service*

Below: 'When it's *Springtime* in Alaska, it's 40 below,' but in the summer it's light all day long. This cabin is well 'dug in'—the better to withstand the harsh Alaskan winter, where temperatures go far below the 'comfort zone.' Cabins left empty are often inhabited by the next trapper, miner or general woodsman who needs shelter. It's etiquette to replenish supplies, leaving good provender for the next inhabitant.

from

THE CALL OF THE WILD

Have you known the Great White Silence, not
  a snow-gemmed twig aquiver?
   (Eternal truths that shame our soothing lies.)
Have you broken trail on snowshoes? mushed
  your huskies up the river,
   Dared the unknown, led the way, and
   clutched the prize?
Have you marked the map's void spaces,
  mingled with the mongrel races,
   Felt the savage strength of brute in every thew?
And though grim as hell the worst is, can you
  round it off with curses?
   Then hearken to the Wild—it's wanting you.

Have you suffered, starved and triumphed,
  groveled down, yet grasped at glory,
   Grown bigger in the bigness of the whole?
'Done things' just for the doing, letting babblers
  tell the story,
   Seeing through the nice veneer the naked soul?
Have you seen God in His splendors, heard the
  text that nature renders?
   (You'll never hear it in the family pew.)
The simple things, the true things, the silent
  men who do things—
   Then listen to the Wild—it's calling you.

     ——*Robert Service*

A wizened Eskimo elder displays the lines of age and a lot of weather in this photo *(above)*, taken near Alaska's Baker Lake, in the eastern continental Northwest Territories. The Eskimo call themselves Inuit, which is their word for 'The People.' Snowshoes, a dog sled and a sturdy tent *(right)* are essentials for winter travel in Canada's Northwest Territories.

THE LIVING BEAUTIES

I never knew, until they went,
How much their laughter really meant.
I never knew how much the place
Depended on each little face;
How barren home could be and drear
Without its living beauties here.

I never knew that chairs and books
Could wear such sad and solemn looks!
That rooms and halls could be at night
So still and drained of all delight.
This home is now but brick and board
Where bits of furniture are stored.

I used to think I loved each shelf
And room for what it was itself.
And once I thought each picture fine
Because I proudly called it mine.
But now I know they mean no more
Than art works hanging in a store.

Until they went away to roam
I never knew what made it home.
But I have learned that all is base,
However wonderful the place
And decked with costly treasures, rare,
Unless the living joys are there.

——*Edgar Guest*

Above: Nuggets and flakes among the gravel? These girls pan for gold on Bonanza Creek, in Alaska's Yukon territory. There's still gold in these creeks, and plenty of loners who seek their 'yellow ruin' with a sluicepan. *Right:* This mischievous scamp with his Cheshire Cat grin crouches in his papa's boat, drawn aground on the shore of Hankin Inlet, in Canada's Northwest Territories. His papa may be a hunter or a trapper, but most definitely a native of the 'Land of the Midnight Sun.'

Below: This Native Canadian, his skin tent pitched on the shore of Baker Lake in the Northwest Territories, has stood the test of tradition.

THE PACIFIC

COAST

NOSTALGIA

I am homesick for the ocean,
For the breakers' mighty roar,
For the waves that chase each other
Toward the sand dunes on the shore.

I would watch the seagulls flying,
I would mark the porpoise leap,
I would see the changing colors
On the ever-changing deep.

I would watch the great ships coming
From strange seas and lands afar,
And pretend, as each reached harbor,
That *my* ship had crossed the bar.

I would watch the sunshine sparkle
On the wave crests' snowy foam—
Oh, I'm homesick for the ocean
And my humble, seaside home!

——*Laura M Gradick*

Previous page: 'Catch a wave and you're sitting on top of the world' go the words of the song as wetsuited surfers paddle out to catch their next 'ride' as the Pacific Ocean breaks toward a northern California beach. *Left:* Strollers pause amid the driftwood on a Pacific beach replete with sun, sand and far horizons. *Above:* Highways of air, sea and land keep the Pacific Coast busy, and the beautiful rock- and wood-strewn beaches are ever becoming acquainted with new pairs of strangers' feet.

from

FOREST HYMN

The groves were God's first temples. Ere man learned
To hew the shaft, and lay the architrave,
And spread the roof above them—ere he framed
The lofty vault, to gather and roll back
The sound of anthems; in the darkling wood,
Amid the cool and silence, he knelt down,
And offered to the Mightiest solemn thanks,
And supplication.

My heart is awed within me, when I think
Of the great miracle that still goes on
In silence, round me—the perpetual work
Of thy creation, finished, yet renewed Forever.

——*William Cullen Bryant*

Left: Bicyclists tour the woodland highways of British Columbia's Vancouver Island, just west across the Georgia Strait from the forests of the mainland. Vancouver Island is a place of forest and field, and a genteel wildness all its own. *Above:* Children of the Quinault tribe balance on logs with an ancient red cedar *(center)* rising up behind them, in Washington, the 'Evergreen State.'

A CYPRESS TREE

A wind-swept cypress tree of Monterey
Is leaning out to catch the ocean's spray;
One branch upraised, another sprawling low,
Are waving in the moon's resplendent glow.

Though but a photogravure of a scene
Presented in a nature magazine,
Some subtle charm, not sighted in the ken,
Impels one to reflect and look again.

———*Willis Hudspeth*

A Monterey cypress leans out from a northern California cliff in this photoportrait *(above)* of a sunset on the 'wide Pacific.'

THE SEA

By the rolling sea, on the wave-beat shore,
Is the place I love when the breakers roar;
When the howling winds drive the angry skies
Till the shadows grow where the sea-gull flies.

When the cloudless sky wears a turquoise hue,
Then the sea replies with a deeper blue;
And its feathery edge a white rim shows
Where the sandy beach in the sunlight glows.

How the moon's soft rays, in the summer night,
On the dimpling waves paint a path of light;
And the stars like diamonds gleam afar,
While the sea sobs low on the harbor bar.

There's never a day and never an hour,
When by the sea, but we feel its power;
And whether its mood be wild or tame,
Its spell is over us just the same.

The years will come and the years will go
While ever its tide will ebb and flow;
And never its breast rest quietly
Till it laps the shore of eternity.

——*Benj F Brown*

A 'surfing safari' has taken this Cadillac owner from Mexico's Baja beaches to the mouth of Waddell Creek on the coast of California's Santa Cruz County. These two fellows *(above)* look for air bubbles during an afternoon of clamming on California's beautifully rocky seacoast.

Above: A man guides his small motorboat around fish traps set by the Quinault Indian tribe, on way his upstream at the mouth of the Quinault River in western Washington state. The spring rainclouds in the sunset are obviously dispersing, since 'red sky at night, sailor's delight.'

SHIPS AT ANCHOR

They know the vagabondage of the seas—
Those ships that swing at anchor in the bay,
With flags that flutter on a lazy breeze
From masts that lean in such a friendly way,
As though they gossiped of that far-gone day
When decks ran flame, and fierce men fought for gold;
Or of great virgin, forest lands, when they
Held their green council in some Arden old;
O, they are wise! those ships that swing at ease,
Home—from the vagabondage of the seas!

These are but poet-fancies—what I hear
Are hawsers straining, and the swish of spray—
A sailor singing, as he mends his gear,
Of lips that lure him back to old Cathay.
We talk of Venice and its barges gay,
Of lurid sunsets over Singapore,
Of pearls, and ports where I may never stray
Who love the sea—and its enchanting lore;
But here, I cull such treasure as I may
From those old ships at anchor in the bay.

——*Alice Marston Seaman*

The harbor at Newport, Oregon *(left and above)* is alive with many of the commercial fishing boats that ply the waters of the Pacific coast. Sport fishing amid the annual salmon run coexists with a commercial fishing industry that continues to thrive, despite hard times in recent years.

OLD CHURCHES

Hast been where the full-blossomed bay-tree is blowing
    With odours like Eden's around?
Hast seen where the broad-leaved palmetto is growing,
    And wild vines are fringing the ground?
Hast sat in the shade of catalpas, at noon,
    And ate the cool gourds of their clime;
Or slept where magnolias were screening the moon,
    And the mocking-bird sung her sweet rhyme?

Ay, pray on thy knees, that each old rural fane
    They have left to the bat and the mole,
May sound with the loud-pealing organ again,
    And the full swelling voice of the soul.
Peradventure, when next thou shalt journey thereby
    Even-bells shall ring out on the air,
And the dim-lighted windows reveal to thine eye
    The snowy-robed pastor at prayer.

——*Arthur Cleveland Coxe*

Above: This old, well-kept church is typical of the treasures one can find, 'just wandering around' the Pacific coastways. The Santa Barbara Church *(at right)* at Randsburg in southern California, is both a landmark and a place of worship.

MY CHILDHOOD HOME

I am thinking today of the 'Old Home'
That stands at the foot of a hill.
'Twas built to make someone happy,
Though sorrow came often to fill
The rooms that were big and old-fashioned,
With furniture simple and old,
But someone who lived there was dearer
Than any fine silver or gold.

My Home! in the old apple orchard,
You seemed like a mansion to me
In the days when I was a youngster
And living so happy and free.
'Twas there that our loved ones would gather,
And oh! the dear friends that we met,
The kind that you like to have near you,
The ones you will never forget.

So often I find myself dreaming,
And sometimes my eyes fill with tears;
I see my dear Mother still waiting
To greet me, as in the past years.
Oh! memories dear ever linger,
Stay with me wherever I roam,
For it is so sweet to remember
The scenes of my dear childhood home.

——*Oleta Fox Cloos*

Above: California's soil is refreshed well and often by coastal fog, a feature which aids California in being the leading agricultural state in the United States. *Right:* This Oregon farmhouse wears its weathered redwood with dignity. Many footsteps have come home to this door, its lilac-fragrant air wafting pungently across memory's fields—a fragrance that means 'grandma,' and says 'return.'

One's fascination with the out-of-the-way places of the North American landscape need not stop at continent's edge: the United States reaches into the Pacific to include the Hawaiian Islands. Here the eastern end of Route 450 on the Island of Moloka'i overlooks Halawa Bay where Moa'ula Stream empties into the azure Pacific.

from
A WHOLESOME SPOT

The weather, seventy degrees,
  With moisture at the happy mean,
Is smiling on a slope of trees
  Of citron, pea and balsam green.

Like boulders, clouds are piling high;
  A narrow gorge of paling blue
Is closing midway in the sky
  As yellow lightning filters through.

A soaring bird now turns and flaps,
  And in the scenery is heard,
With distant, softened thunder claps,
  The medley of a mocking bird.

The sweetest berries ever grown
  Are ripening and gone to waste,
And not a mountaineer has known
  An evil substance in their taste.

The tourist lingers to imbibe
  The wholesomeness that here abounds
And makes, which he cannot describe,
  A snakeless Eden of the grounds.

——*Willis Hudspeth*

Above: Coconut plantations in Hawaii made many an individual's fortune in bygone years. These days, they're mainly corporate affairs, or simply adornments for the state's country roads. *Right:* This rustic bungalow, with its garden and outbuildings, could be that 'little bit of paradise' that the careworn pilgrim has been seeking.

On the southern loop of Highway 11, the pleasant little village of Na'alehu *(below)*, on the island of Hawaii, claims the honor of being the southernmost village in the entire United States.

OUTWARD BOUND

The estuary surges with a raft
   Of ferry boats and liners, yachts and tugs,
   A man-of-war, floats crawling slow as slugs,
And fleets of various other masted craft.
Our hoarsely whistling steamer stirs abaft;
   The engine throbs; the vessel creaks, and lugs
   Its wedge-shaped prow around a pier, then chugs
A foaming fissure from its heavy draft.

                —*Willis Hudspeth*

Completed in 1936 during the halcyon days of WPA, this bridge *(below)* bears US Route 101 across the Yaquina River at Newport, Oregon—where the river meets the ocean, and the little boats set out upon the wide Pacific. US Route 101 'up the coast,' or US route 20 'over from Corvallis,' will get you there.

THE NEXT GENERATION

We shall leave you many problems; many tasks we
    couldn't do.
We shall leave a world unfinished that shall need the
    best of you,
And I wonder as I see you grouped in school and
    college still,
If you know the chance that waits you in the places
    you must fill.

The voice of opportunity is calling loud for men;
Men of wisdom, men of courage, to set right the
    world again;

Men of honor, men of vision; men the future's work
    to share;
And I wonder if you've heard it, and have started
    to prepare.

We have blundered; we have stumbled and have
    somehow lost our way.
In the wreckage of our failures we are gropers all
    today,
But you boys who follow after face a future strewn
    with need
And endless opportunities to conquer and succeed.

——*Edgar Guest*

Above: Californians in the summer of their youth scamper among the dunes, on a sunny Pacific coastal beach near California Highway 1—which follows the most extensive state coastline in the continental US. *Right:* As children through the ages have taken tentative steps along the road of life, these children walk hand in hand on a sun-dappled path in California's Big Basin State Park—dwarfed by the huge California redwoods, they are nonplussed but undaunted by the presence of such great age and size. In the light and shadow, their path along this country road is, for them, headed towards a bright future—'Happy Trails,' indeed.